TABLE OF CONTENTS

INTRODUCTORY SOLUTIONS

This Book Is Dedicated to:

My Family. My future Deana, Ant, and Kaz. My Legacy, My past, Shakur, Ellazena Ways, and Ellazena Blake. Also, the People of Camden, NJ

Together we "Cando" Anything

WE ARE ONE PEOPLE, ONE FAMILY, WITH ONE PURPOSE AND MISSION:

TO BUILD OUR COMMUNITY

This Publication provides the Author's opinion in regards to the subject matter contained herein. The Publisher/Author [Anthony Ways) does not intend with this publication, to render professional, legal advice.

The Publisher/Author disclaims any personal liability, loss or risk incurred as a consequence of the use and application, either directly or indirectly, of any advice, information or methods presented herein.

While none of these stories in this book are fabricated, some of the names and details may have been changed to protect the privacy of the individuals mentioned. Although the author, co-authors, and publisher have made every effort to ensure that they information in this book was correct at press time, the author and publisher do not assume and herby disclaim any liability to any party for any loss, damage, or disruption caused by errors or omissions, whether such errors or omissions result from negligence, accident, or any other cause.

The Journey:
Decriminalizing Black America
Volume 1

By: Anthony Ways

ABOUT THIS PAMPHLET

Since the Blacks arrival into America the Black community has been enslaved, ruled, and dominated by outside forces. This application continues today by the criminalization of our youth. The choice of weapon had been, and continue to be the "Law". One example is the disparity in the drug laws between crack cocaine and powder cocaine. Possession of (5 grams) of crack cocaine (in poor black communities) will get the same amount of prison time that possession of (500 grams) of powder cocaine holders (rich white guys in board rooms).

This pamphlet and the series of pamphlets to follow will address this reality of "criminalizing" Black people head on. First by reviewing the author's persecution by this system although he is **ABSOLUTELY INNOCENT**. Then by reviewing the social-political-economic structure that breeds this destructive reality.

The pamphlets that will follow will address each subject in-depth, and at the end of each series there will be practical applications on how to address a different "issue". This will be the "HOW TO" chapter at the end of each pamphlet.

Before addressing the issue in this pamphlet I want to begin with a statement from P.W. Botha, taken from a speech delivered in 1985. Addressed to his "beloved White Afrikaners".

"...By now every one of us has seen it practically that the blacks cannot rule themselves. **Give them guns and they will kill each other.** They are good in nothing else but making noise, dancing, marrying many wives and indulging in sex.... Let us all accept that the Black man is the symbol of poverty, mental inferiority, laziness and emotional incompetence.

...Our experts should work day and night to set the Black man against his fellow man. His inferior sense of morals can be exploited beautifully. And here is a creature that lacks foresight.... **The average Black does not plan his life beyond a year..."**

THESE ARE THE VIEWS OF THOSE WHO SEEK TO DESTROY US. LET'S BUILD.

CHAPTER 1

A JOURNEY TO PROVE MY INNOCENCE

On April 23, 1989, two Caucasian men by the name of Wayne Hunter and John Weist we're getting high off of drugs and alcohol at a party in Haddon Township, when both decided to drive into the city of Camden to purchase cocaine. Their decision on that fateful night changed my life forever.

Hunter and Weist drove up to two black men in the dark of night and solicited the purchase of drugs on the corner of Louis and Thurmond st. [this is a point of contention because the state declares it occurred on Louis and Chase st.] It is not exactly clear what happened at that point, speculation is that a robbery ensued, and one of the black men produced a gun and shot Weist once in the torso. Weist, died as a result of a single gunshot.

The following day Bryant Anderson and myself were arrested and charged with first-degree murder in the Weist shooting. Subsequently a trial was conducted with a jury finding of Anderson [co-defendant] having been innocent of all charges, and myself being wrongfully convicted and sentenced to life imprisonment, for [murder] a crime that I did not commit and knew nothing about.

During the preliminary investigation of this crime by Homicide Detectives and Investigators from the Prosecutor Office. An elaborate frame-up began to take shape fingering my co-defendant and myself as the persons who committed the crime. The frame-up began with the only eye-witness to the crime Wayne Hunter who was in the car with Weist when he was shot and killed. Homicide Detective and Prosecutor Investigators, paraded a photographic array [photo-line-up] before the witness, the twist was that my photograph was the only picture shown to the witness with a "hat" on, because it was said that one of the perpetrators wore a hat. This is significant because science have proven that Caucasians are less likely to identify Blacks especially high on drugs and in the middle of a crime. Predictably my photograph was picked out by the witness as being one of the perpetrators of the shooting. In the jurisprudence of the law; such a prejudicial line-up is not only illegal, but also inadmissible in a court of law [trial].

You'd say well that is a very flimsy case. So did Homicide Detectives and Prosecuting Investigators. One because it fails to implicate my [co-defendant] and secondly because they knew their actions with the photo-line-up were illegal.

With the passage of a few weeks and no additional evidence, Detective Latham went about creating and fabricating evidence to support the trumped-up charges against me. He recruited a young drug addicted black female named Donna Carter to identify [co-defendant] and myself falsely as the perpetrators of this crime.

Needing to develop more conclusive evidence, these people in their Diabolical thinking blackmailed this black female into making the false accusation that she witnessed [co-defendant] and myself approach that car on the night in question, with the inference that we'd committed the shooting. Which turns out to be an outright utterance that was fabricated due to police threats and pressure. All of which the witness Donna Carter revealed as she set on the witness stand during a post-trial proceeding.

It was learned [after] our trial that Ms. Carter was given drugs by the Camden police and was not prosecuted on prostitution charge(s) in return for falsely submitting [written] statements identifying [co-defendant] and myself as co-conspirators and the persons who committed the crime of murder that fatal evening.

The evidence against me consisted of 1) Hunter identifying my photograph in a line-up shown to him by detective Latham. This line up being a complete sham. **I was the only person in the line-up wearing a hat!** And 2) Donna Carter a drug user who was given drugs by these detectives to make false statements.

Numerous witnesses have statements on my behalf that I was at a party on the night and time that the crime was committed. Thereby making it physically impossible for me to have been present let alone a participant in this crime. However the primary Homicide Detective investigating this particular homicide detective "Latham" chose not to believe any of my witnesses because I had already been named as a suspect and the ball had started rolling!!.

Eyewitnesses who saw the incident came forward two days after the crime and named Frank King and Ben Johnson as the perpetrators, but Detective Latham chose to reject these eyewitnesses because of Hunters faulty photo identification.

While detained at the Camden County Jail prior to my posting bail on these charges. Concerned community citizens, and friends who knew me to be innocent went around town asking questions about the murder. Talking to the eyewitnesses who were rejected by Detective Latham, they gathered information, people in the community conducted a citizen's arrest, and took this man Frank King to the home of a known and respected black police detective who lives in the black community.

That black detective through questioning (at his home) obtained information from Mr. King that led to him to believe that King was involved in this murder and that the wrong man had been arrested. Therefore, he took that information to police Detective Latham, and the prosecutor, but he was told in no uncertain terms to essentially mind his business and to disregard the information he'd obtained through questioning Frank King.

At my trial, Mr. King admitted being in possession of a .44 caliber handgun on the night of the murder, the same caliber gun used in the crime. His crime partner Ben Johnson pleaded the Fifth to protect himself against self-incrimination.

My co-defendant was acquitted of all charges, and I was found guilty by a jury who heard the same testimony and evidence against me as they heard against my alleged co-conspirator. You figured that out!

I was railroaded and subsequently sentenced to a term of life imprisonment and everyone involved in the case knows I'm innocent.

You can read more about my trial on my website at: www.AthonywaysJourney.com

My case has been appealed, and my conviction affirmed by the N.J. Appellate Division. The Appellate Division was misled about the prejudicial line-up and what role the suggestibility of myself being the only person in the photo array (photo line-up) who was the only person with a hat on, and the significant feature that hat played in the line-up. The shooter was said to have had on a hat when the shooting took place. The appellate

Court misinterpreted that the trial Judge had properly assessed the illegal photo lineup during what is known as a 'Wade Hearing', but the trial judge did not. The details are covered on the web site.

After my trial my family hired private investigators, who have found conclusive evidence that proves my innocence. That evidence was presented at a Post-Conviction Relief Hearing. But the presiding judge denied my application. Why? Was it rubber stamped? Was it a protection of the prosecutor's conviction? You be the judge. Here is a summary of the evidence.

AT THE PCR HEARING

Mrs. Carter testified to her motivation for testifying falsely stating that she had a record, and that she was a part-time prostitute at the time. Also being charged with soliciting a police officer, and getting arrested. She went on to state on the witness stand that; she gave her children to her mother after being caught in crack houses throughout the city of Camden by police officers. Stating that she'd been in and out of the county jail maybe 15 or 16 times. Admittedly been picked up on Admiral Wilson Boulevard for prostitution and caught with drugs on her. Mrs. Carter stated on the witness stand before the P.C.R judge that she'd been approached by the prosecutor, while high on drugs, to falsely and knowingly persuade Mrs. Carter to finger me as one of the guys who approached the murder victim's car that night. Mrs. Carter went on to say on the witness stand that when the prosecutor made that statement, that statement did not come from Donna Carter (referring to the false testimony that the prosecutor had her make). She went on to say that he (prosecutor) knew a lot of things about me [her] because he told me my back history… At the time all i really wanted to do was use [referring to drugs]. I didn't want to get locked up for nothing and nobody". Donna Carter stated on the witness stand "… that because she <u>has been sober for two years</u> she came forward to clear her conscious by correcting a wrong that she took part in and to tell the truth. She testified that she lied in her statement and at trial because she was told "what to say". Concluding by stating "I never seen appellant [myself] at no murder scene".

Kyle Young

The prosecutor and Detective Latham attempted to elicit a false statement from Young that I was on the corner of Chase street the so-called crime scene, [evidence have shown that the murder did not even happen there], but Young refused to lie. The Detective arrested and locked him up for a few days to scare him, however he held his ground.

Hall the Black Detective

Hall testified while in his residence, King stated to him "I'm not the only one in Camden with a .44 Magnum". Prior to King's volunteered comment, Hall was unaware that a .44 Magnum was utilized in the homicide and stated the type of weapon used was not public knowledge.

T. Williams

Mr. Williams testified that Frank King came to him on the night of April 23, 1989 [the night of the murder] and wanted to sell him a gun. So King took him on the side of Mr. Williams's house and showed him a .44 Magnum. Mr. Williams ask King if there were any bodies on it, and King said, "yes, I shot somebody earlier", Mr. Williams at that time declined to buy the gun from King.

Thomas Ways

My cousin had a conversation with Mr. King wherein King admitted to him that he committed the crime, and that "he wanted to do the right thing knowing that [I] didn't have anything to do with it, knowing he [I] was an innocent man". Stating that "he's gonna come forward and tell that he committed the crime".

Frank King

King was called to testify. Unaware of the legal requirements to overturn a conviction, Mr. King made an attempt to clear me. King testified that when he was in the custody of Detective Hall, he took them to an area where "he secured the .44 - caliber gun". He explained "its safe to say that there wasn't too many of those running around in Camden.

King replied on the witness stand to the prosecutors inquiries by stating the he [King] had confessed in the past to killing John Weist. However in open court he would deny being the killer. But continued to stress that appellant [I] did not commit the murder. The court inquired whether King knew the identity of the killer and King stated, "**Someone else did it. It wasn't [appellant] and yes, I do know who did it". Throughout his testimony, King repeated his awareness that appellant [I] had served "a decade in jail for a crime he didn't commit". Going on to state: ... "I'm caught in the middle, you know... I mean, I know the man didn't do it. I know who did it. All right? I mean, I'm not gonna implicate - - all I can say is that I know this man didn't do it".**

All this New Evidence along with other testimony on the many legal violations was not enough for this judge. He denied me relief. WHY?!

There is no creditable evidence against me. Mr. King jeopardized his own freedom and attempted to inform the system of his wrong. Donna Carter, Detective Hall, and Kyle Young with others made it clear that the prosecutor team was singled minded in prosecuting this case and went as far as framing me to get a conviction. To arrogant to correct this wrong and injustice against me, because this is not a question of justice to them. In fact they care less, it is about securing a conviction and to hell with justice and the overwhelming evidence that proves my innocence.

How is it that righteous citizens, professionals, school teachers, and others in the arm forces can come into court and testify that I was with them on the night in question, and that there was no way I could have committed this crime and they not be believed?

How is it that Eyewitnesses to the murder can come into court and testify with indisputable accuracy that they witnessed the murder and that Mr. Ways was not the killer and in fact Mr. King was, and still not be believed?

How is it possible That Mr. King who has been identified by others can come into court and state he knows who the killer is that it is not Mr. Ways Coupled with him stating he did have a .44 magnum that night, that he did try to sell it that night after shooting someone, and that he confessed to the murder on many occasions, but still not be believed?

Maybe the answer is in Kyle Young's, Detective Halls, and Donna Carter's subsequent testimony of Detective Latham's singled mindlessness to convict me? Or is the answer in the White guys identification of me in that sham photo array?

Only in America can one White guys testimony stating I "resemble the shooter" not that I am the shooter, but that I "resemble the shooter" is more creditable than the multiple testimony of these black people who clearly demonstrated my innocence.

These questions and the fact that I am living in this nightmare leads me to write this pamphlet.

In my struggle throughout the years I looked for the answers of how it was possible that an entire city can know of my innocence yet a hand full of outsiders can come into our community under the cloak of Law, and kidnap me and nothing can be done about it?

Please continue to read and analyze my findings.

CHAPTER 2

POLITICS AND LAW

In the discourse of sharing the biographical history of my trial, my conviction, and my innocence, I've laid bare what had almost become a common set of facts and circumstances in the conviction of many innocent Black Men languishing in prisons protesting our innocence, and fighting against the odds; a judicial system that seem to be impartial to the obvious injustices woven into the American System. We have only to look at the many cases discovered of innocent men released from America's Death-Rows; the Multiple cases that DNA evidence has exonerated and restored innocent men their freedom; to understand the distinct challenges of my own case.

The confession of several young black men in the vicious assault and rape in the infamous "Central Park Rape Case"; confessions from the outset said to have been coerced, and brutalized from those young men by police; are suddenly revealed after thirteen years to have been illegally extracted from those young teenagers at the time. This is not exaggerated or an isolated case of mistaken identity. Because the single perpetrator of the crime has come forward and confessed; DNA evidence [blood & hair samples] clearly supports the confessor's enactment of the actual crime.

How can such atrocities take place? Why do they take place? In seeking answers to these and many other questions, I am committed to share some of my findings with you the reader.

In America's governmental structure, the three (3) branches of government [legislative, executive, and the Judiciary] are the infrastructure that "the powers that be" use to implement their control, and dominance over, and in our communities.

In looking specifically at the legislative branch [Senate and the House of representative], we will observe that it is those Representatives' who are responsible for the actual writing and composing of the laws of the land; which in theory are supposed to protect and represent the rights of the citizens of this country; However in practice specifically for Blacks that theory is tomfoolery. The reality is that the primary function of this branch of government is to protect the rights and property of the ruling class.

With a more critical observation, we discover that all laws are not created by Congress [per se], but are composed, formulated, and decreed, into legislation, by partisan politicians, by interest groups, such as Corporations, Think Tanks, Technological Institutes, and the Prison Industrial Complex's just to name a few. It is Corporations and Institutes whom by-an-large structure the intricate yet tangled-web of laws that govern our society, at the Federal and State levels.

Findings complied in extensive Reports, and Scientific Studies are just some of the tools used to sway policy-makers to enact Laws that are beneficial and profitable to some of the interest groups mentioned above.

One such policy created by an "interest group" that was enacted into law by Congressional Legislation is the "Crime Bill", and the so-called "War on Drugs". Case studies were conducted by Social Workers, and leading Psychologist & Sociologist in the field who created Marginalized Reports & findings which alleged that Black males between the ages of 11 to 35 are inept, dangerous, and a menace to society. Thereby persuading Federal & State Legislators to enact more stringent laws to support a "War on Crime" in the United States, and throughout each independent state.

As a part of their propaganda efforts for support of the "Crime Bill" [code for: war on black men particular & Black People in general] these policy & law makers' provoked fear into the public by referring to Black Males as "Predators" through newspapers, wire-services, magazines, and evening news sound-bites. At the same time effectively creating an atmosphere for a police occupational force in our communities 'Targeting' Black people all over the country.

Which then lead to the next phase of this campaign known as the "war on crime" which brings the Executive branch of government into the picture. Essentially the Executive branch of government job is to make its citizens "white folks feel secure" again by enforcing these types of corrupt, bankrupt, dominating policies over so-called minority [Black & Hispanic] communities.

Through the direction of the President of the United States on the Federal level, the Governor in the state level, and the Mayor on the city level, they send out their Attorney Generals [who direct Prosecutors] and Law Enforcers [the F.B.I., State Troopers, and local Police] to kidnap, imprison, and at times KILL "the threat" [Blacks from the age of 11 to 35] under the guise of community protection & National Security.

In evaluating my case, you will find that it was the Executive branch of government [Detective Latham and the Prosecutor] that framed me, and imprisoned me by using self-hatched and fabricated evidence. It was them who made the decision on whom to believe and whom not to believe; It was them that decided to put that sham of a photo array together, It was them that gave Donna Carter drugs to effectuate false accusations against me, but this is no new policy against young Black People. We have been declared enemies of the state as far back as the sixties when our parents were marching and fighting for Civil & Human Rights, and Self-Determination.

The F.B.I. director J. Edgar Hoover infamous for creating a prototype policy against Black People in the 60s known as the CoIntelPro [Counterintelligence Program] a program with the expressed purpose of falsely imprisoning many law abiding citizens, activist, and black leaders. This was a tactical application for our destruction. Geronimo Pratt comes to mind as an example. The same atmosphere was created and enforced by police & prosecutors then, as now. Allowing for a rash of police shootings throughout the country and killings of these black males, shot for reaching to get his identification, killed for selling cigarettes or CDs. The word Genocide comes to mind when viewed in its proper light.

However the systematic murdering of a target people can cause unrest and civil protest by citizens in the communities resulting in a loss of confidence in the government and its Federal & State agencies. Therefor shrewd policies & laws have to be an enacted & enforced through completed 'net works' of indoctrination's to forestall civil disobedience by in our community. In addition, "The Powers that be" have to create an image throughout the international community of a democracy & patriotism in this country in order to induce this style of government in other nations, this is how they implement their "One World order" agenda of Imperialism. You see with a democracy, "the Powers that be" can replace governments every four (4) years keeping foreign leaders aligned to their program without firing a single bullet. In essence in acting control & domination in the world under U.S. hegemony and under the disguise of seeking peace & cooperation from both its citizens and the World.

So if the policy on Black youth consisted solely of shooting first, they would not emerge in the eyes of its citizens or the World as democratic & fair peace-keepers. Instead they've become adept at implementing policies that encourage & support false imprisonment instead. Falsely accusing and imprisoning black males has almost become an accepted norm, so much so that when these cases are revealed for their falsities there is hardly any outcry, alarm, or condemnation by the communities at large and most effected by the countless injustices that occur against our own people. There exist a hush & silence so pervasive that it actually aids & abets the government agencies that in fact does perpetrate such monstrous acts of cruelty.

And through the third branch of government, the Judicial branch [The Court System] which is supposed to interpret the laws written by Congress, however as we descriptively noted Congress is a tool of "the powers that be" [Corporate Executives & Interest Groups] who are behind the scenes writing the laws. The unveiling of the indirect control "the powers that be" have over the judicial branch of government makes it crystal clear why my absolute innocence was not enough to secure my freedom. The standing policy if that Black youths are a menace to this society regardless of guilt or innocence, and therefore, the courts onus was/is to imprison Blacks from the ages of 11 to 35 for as long as possible. The end-result is not only the criminalizing of our community, but the victimization of Black people, in general, and Black youth in particular.

The clearest historical example of the Courts policy towards Blacks were written by the United States Supreme Court in 1857 which ruled in the Dred Scott decision that Black people were not human beings, but instead ⅗ human, declaring our people the property of the [Money Lords].

This policy is still crafted in the constitution in a cunning way.

The 13th Amendment of the American constitution states "neither slavery nor involuntary servitude, except as a <u>PUNISHMENT FOR CRIME WHEREFORE THE PARTY SHALL HAVE BEEN DULY CONVICTED</u>, shall exist within the United States, or any place subject to their jurisdiction."

At first glance it appears that this amendment totally ends slavery, but a closer look reveals that slavery was not abolished 100% only modified from one form to another [Chattel Slavery to Wage Slavery]. This Amendment makes it clear that at any time Congress can create laws that makes numerous behaviors crimes punishable by imprisonment "a life of enslavement".

This continued racist policy is written in the drug laws of today punishing Black users 20 times more severe than White users. Sending our children to prison as adults, declaring, "lock em up now, and throw away the key because they will be future 'predators'". And the list of these pernicious laws goes on. The "Rule of Law" is one of the keys to this country's power. For over Four Hundred years America had been using slavery to Jim Crow, and now criminalizing the black youth. The facts show that three out of four Black youths in this country will be under the system [Slave House] in their lifetime.

Our youth have been facing a life journey that are full of many traps that leads to imprisonment in which by adulthood they will become fully engulfed in, unless we change this destructive reality that is a part of the social-political-economic strategy of "the Powers that be".

The observation of this strategy reveals that regardless of our guilt or innocence, most of us will be criminalized and to those who have not forgotten me know that this process had me lingering in prison. I submit that this systematic defeating scenario [modern day slavery] must be fought with vigor.

WE HAVE TO BRING AN END TO THIS EFFECTIVE PLAN IMPLEMENTED AGAINST US. Because this system has been, and continue to be used toward our destruction.

Which leads to the question of what we can do about our plight of being criminalized as a people?

My fight and continued struggle to prove my innocence has brought me to a place of understanding that only the acquisition of "Power" can change the reality. "True liberty does not rest on legal or moral rights, but on the control of the government's bureaucracy and courts that apply these complex rules and regulations." It is the writing of Statues and laws where we have to become formidable.

From my position, being the controller of our own destiny is the true definition of empowerment [Power], and it starts with self-observation, that addresses our social realities in our communities starting first with ourselves.

Power has to be addressed in the political arena, i.e. changing the policies that are in place for our destruction. And power has to be addressed by our input and control over the economic infrastructure in and around our communities creating ownership of property. To be masters of the hands we are dealt, we will have to develop knowledge in the tactics used against us that control our lives, and develop counter structures to defeat the Law as it now stands, by destroying the laws of the land that are harmful.

CHAPTER 3
SELF EMPOWERMENT

Who has the POWER? How does a declaration of war declared upon our community go unchecked? How it is possible that an entire city can know of my innocence yet a hand full of outsiders in the name of the law, can come and kidnap me from my community and nothing can be done about it?

This reality leads us to further questions of how are we going to prevent known injustices in our communities? How do we take control of ourselves, and our communities? What is the foundation that must be laid for change to be made? And if it is through "POWER ", what is power and how do we obtain it? How do we empower ourselves and each other? And how do we remove the occupiers out of our communities?

According to Rollo May, "Power is essential for all living things. Man, in particular, cast on this barren crust of earth years ago with the hope he survives, finds he must use his powers and confront opposing forces at every point in his struggle with the earth and with his fellow man."

According to Dr. Wilson, "power refers to the ability to do, the ability to be, and the ability to prevail. "Powerless is to be without a Will, lifeless, without effect or influence; to be nothing and of no account.

Are we exercising Power, or is power being exercised upon us in our communities?

The answer can only come by knowing where does power derive from and where did it begin?
We have been taught that "In the beginning was the word" or said differently, "the beginning of everything is thought".

Our thoughts must be wrapped in words in order to mentally process it. So that leads us to the conclusion that the beginning of everything are words. And if words (thoughts) are the beginning, then every word we speak or think have power, that is each idea, each thought, and each mental image gives us power to do.

Therefore our way of life, our physical conditions, and our environment shows what we habitually think. (What does out environment say about us?)

Because we are creatures of habits in our mind, and in our bodies, the beginning stages to change "and change is a must" is to change the habitual negative thoughts in our minds, therein replacing those thoughts with more creative productive, and faithful thoughts, herein acquiring power. But change has to first start in our minds.

It is in the mind that we have to evaluate who and what we are. What and who "the powers that be" are. Who and what we intend to become, and what strategy we must use to be victorious in our mission. This is accomplished through the endowments of self-awareness, self-discipline, and self-control.

As pointed out by covey," self-awareness is an endowment unique to the human race." It gives us the ability to take inventory of our thoughts, our way of life and our daily actions. Here we can assess our approach to life measuring if we are productive, or if we are counterproductive to our own self-interest. With a deeper question of if we are assisting the enemy's plans, or are we creating and following our own plans.

To be discipline, is to be a disciple to a teaching, a way of life, and or a plan of action.

To be discipline is to live out this way of life to the exclusion of everything else particularly anything that is in opposition to your purpose and therein your plan of action. Self-discipline is practice on two levels which are in the mind and in the body, then a person's ways and actions will reflect the self-discipline created in both realities.

In the mind, we have to script the brain with the instructions on how to conduct ourselves by feeding it desirable foods. This "food" consist of creative and productive ideas, positive emotions, and magnetic thoughts. Using our imagination, and our ambitions, our subconscious, and our desires as tools to fertilize our internal being, using discipline we are planting the seeds "script/plan/idea" within our thought process to be materialized into the physical world.

Our Ways and actions are the practical side of mental creation. It calls for persistence and being ruthless in order to live according to a teaching or way of life decided upon. Carrying on despite of oppositions and obstacles until our goals are obtained. Living the life of a warrior until victory is in hand.

In the application of self-control, it is imperative that we recognize our enemy is a master of psychology and have many elements of power. Being fully aware of this, we must know that we will be confronted on many levels. They will come at us in the realm of pleasure (material gain, sex, and drugs, etc...) with others, they will use the fear tactics of threats, imprisonment, and death, and of course they will use the age old tactic of divide and conquer, using these destructive tactics along the lines of ideology, .our faith and the like.

Force is a tool the powers that be will use on occasions. Its purpose is terroristic in nature, it is used to send us a message of his power (police brutality), and however he will only use massive force as a last resort. Through self-control we can counter all of these psychological games.

In self-awareness, we write the script. In self-discipline, we live out the script, and in self-control, we manage the script avoiding the many traps that are placed in our communities.

With these principles in mind and the use of them as instruments, we are led to the question in this pamphlet. **How   do   we   empower   ourselves?**

SELF EMPOWERMENT?

Our being brothers and sisters essentially are made up of four dimensions which are spiritual, mental, emotional, and physical. If we want to be vigorous, proficient, and productive in our lives, we must as a rule of law develop, expand, and hone each dimension of our being on a daily bases. This   is   the   strength   of   self-discipline.

THE SPIRITUAL DIMENSION:

> The spiritual part of ourselves is our root, it is where we will develop our value system and our code of conduct. It is our connection to the all mighty creator "GOD", from it, all things flow. It is here where the old negative counter-productive scripts that were giving to us during slavery.

These old submission ideas, "begging for a fair chance" must be erased. On the other side of the spectrum, it is here that we must recognize and embrace the positive values that has been passed down to us from generations before us and put them to practical use. And finally, it is in this dimension that we need to come up with fresh ideas that address our circumstances of today's reality.

So if we sow, or allow negative destructive seeds into our spirit, we will create self-destructive, and self-defeating conditions. In the opposite direction, if we sow creative, Constructive, positive life force seeds into our spirit, we will create heaven here on earth, we will accomplish all that we set out to accomplish, long life, independence, freedom, acquiring homes, etc... This is the law of GOD. We reap what we sow or ALLOWED SOWN INTO US.

THE MENTAL DIMENSION

Developing the mind is connected to being in tune to your spirit. Some argue that it is the mind that had to be developed first in order to reach, and understand the spirit. Others make the argument that all things has to first come from the spirit, (a do or die conviction) and then flow outward through the mind and to the physical world, I believe they are both true and necessary on different levels, but whatever your position the mind must be developed which is a multi-task exercise. For now know that we must create a consciousness of confidence, of success, and of collective work, and through our subconscious mind we must condition our lives in exact accord with what we would have it to do, or to be. Again self-awareness will be vital in our development of the mind.

EMOTIONAL DIMENSION:

In the emotional dimension we have to address our emotions within ourselves in order to maximize our ability to create. We have to address our emotions for our ability to interact with the world at large, but more importantly our interaction with our people, community, and team.

Note that it is the psychological emotional pitfalls that are effectively used against us to control and destroy us that is: fear, doubt, hate, jealousy, and envy which are energies behind all that is negatively created. These negative emotions will bring fourth that which you allow to occupy your mind, so if you fear your opponent's power, you will submit to it. If you envy another man's wealth, you will never acquire that wealth in which you envied. If you have doubt in your abilities, then you will accomplish nothing.

Instead occupy your mind with enthusiasm and that in which you are enthused about will be attracted to you.

When you seek to create something that seems impossible, create with faith, this ingredient with others will bring to you that which you so deeply believe in. (To be empowered is to be the controller of your own destiny).

PHYSICAL DIMENSION:

In this dimension, we must rise above the ordinary plane of cause and effect by becoming CAUSERS (in controlling our communities) instead of effectors (as we have been by allowing others to control our communities). This is the power that I am addressing throughout this pamphlet. That we have the ability to be causers, and not just the play toy of "the powers that be".

In order to carry out our mission, we must be at our best, and this include our physical condition. That means we have to eat healthy, and exercise on a regular bases. We have to take time out for relaxation, and finding that place of peace.

In exercising this means building endurance, flexibility, and strength. It is accomplished by jogging, practicing yoga, and or stretching exercises, along with muscle resistant exercise like weight lifting. Military training, martial arts, and the like. In our plans of action, we must write in our script these components for our master mind team.

IN OUR MASTER MIND TEAM:

Defining these dimension as a collective whole, the "physical "is addressed in terms of acquiring the cash we need to build our economic infra-structure.

The "Mental" is addressed by acknowledging, developing, and using our talents for the benefit for ourselves and our community as a whole.

The "Emotional "dimension is addressed with our effective communication and interaction with our Community and our mastermind team. To harness enough E-Motion (energy in motion) together to see our mission through.

The "Spiritual "is addressed when we serve our community, when we provide for our families, and when we leave our sons and daughters a legacy they can build upon.

Hence power is derived from the four dimensions of existence. From these dimensions flows our ability to act, execute, and prevail. First through ourselves than through our mastermind team.

So in recognizing the many traps in our communities, specifically for our youth, we have to identify and create the responses of these traps. Herein, we will begin a journey that will lead us to a new reality.

Then we will be able to practice the other half of this process which is our personal responsibilities to empower ourselves and each other. This empowerment begins again with self. That is : self-awareness, self-discipline, and self-control which then leads to political and economic Power.

It is past time for us to minimize the control, the power, and the influence "the powers that be" have over and in our communities. By taking total control of our thinking process, of our lives, and our commitment to each other, we will undertake a script that will see our mission successfully completed for ourselves and our community.

The universal laws that we will follow to create a new reality will be discussed in greater detail in later released pamphlets, but the point made here is that the first step for "POWER" starts with self-I.e., our thoughts/words.

CHAPTER 4
BUILDING WEALTH TO ACQUIRE POWER

Some may ask what does money have to do with "The Rule of Law" and others may ask how the acquisition of wealth related to my guilt or innocence is. My answer is: "True liberty does not rest on legal or moral rights, but the control of the government's bureaucracy and the courts that apply their complex rules and regulations."

My question is:
How do we acquire the "Power" to control?

Economic power is the power to decide what will be produced, how much it will cost, how many people will be employed, what their wages will be, what the price of goods and services will be, what profit will be made, how these profits will be distributed, and how fast the economy will grow (Dye, 1983).

The dominance over and subordination of our communities are established by the power derived from the ownership and control of property, resources, and the means of production. **This reality causes us to submit to the demands of the power that be as a condition to feed our families.** It is this dominance over our community that must be changed and the rapid accumulation of wealth [capital & property], which equates to Power "by any means necessary" must be our goal, and mission to bring about this change.

If we accept the premise that we are in a state of economic belligerency, as strategic thinkers, we must formulate plans to capture our internal markets from the occupiers, and then proceed to the regional levels controlling production facilities, and the markets throughout those areas. Working towards the long term goal of producing and distributing on the national and international level.

But before we can reach the global markets, we must defend our local markets by stopping the penetration of other people and groups into our communities.

These other people achieve a good deal of economic prosperity at the expense of our community. Stated differently by Fusfeld and Bates, "the entire economy outside of the ghetto benefits from the income capital, and manpower resources that are drawn out, just as it benefits from a pool of low-wage labor that provides relatively low cost services to those outside."

We must change this subordinated role we are taking part in against the invaders, who have used our communities like vipers and suck the blood [our resources] from us by using our labor for pennies, and then turn around and take back those pennies through their grocery stores, through their housing charging outrageous rents, and through their retail shops that take our consumer dollars to build their communities.

It is this same subordination that allow the injustices under "The Rule of Law" to be practiced upon our youth, and in my direct case to remove me from my community without the vitality to resist.

We must change this and begin to invest in our own infrastructure, institutions, and production facilities which creates a power base.

The script must be constructed in ways to implement, teach, and practice the skills on a massive but productive bases. Our loyalty, cooperation, and responsibility for each other and to each other at all times must be the controlling rules. Then embodied in the role as warriors, defend our rights, and defend our markets by being ruthless and persistent in acquiring "Power" i.e, in building wealth, influencing politics, in controlling commerce, and in strategic thinking and it's practical application.

This is an example of what I am attempting to shine the light on in this pamphlet. We must create, own, and operate several systems if we are to be an independent and powerful community, this will begin to bring an end of the domination, and control that others have over our lives. It will also end the criminalization of our people because we will influence the policies via. The law writers, but the systems must not be limited. We must have our influence in schools, publishing books, technology, Banking, agriculture, industrial plants, and the information age, with coding and creating apps. Here we are expressing our talent in new and creative ways.

INVESTORS POINT OF VIEW

If wealth and power via. The control of our communities is the defined mission, we must invest in each other's enterprises. The objective must be collective economics. Creating our own banking system. Be it formal or informal, those that are stable must pool their resources together to give assistance to the young growth companies. The up and coming companies must patronize the establish suppliers from our communities. Investing into each other's business ventures, investing in school & training programs, and growth oriented businesses must be our clear objective.

It is only through investing the earned income back into the collective economic structure that we can convert this money into wealth which is used as a tool of "Power". Using the principle of compound interest, and collective capitalism, we will multiply our growth potential within decades which could have taken generations under other conditions. So focusing our energy in the sections of business, and investing. We will be creating business systems, and investing our capital gain back into these systems. This is where our community will find long term wealth and success. With wealth, the growth of our influence upon the "Rule of Law" will become apparent.

The details of an economic package will be published in later series of this pamphlet. We will grow!

CHAPTER 5
ACQUIRING POLITICAL POWER

Since we know that we don't have the means to conquer at this present time, we have to take a defensive posture of waiting until we are stronger. In recognizing that we are in defense mode, the next step is to create a plan of action. In a defensive posture, we can adopt many tactical techniques. One such technique is "the mirror reflection". In this tactic, we infiltrate the system and reflect back to them what they do. This way they can't figure out our strategy.

This is best employed in politics. When you do what your opponent does, following their actions as best as possible, they can't figure you out and they are blinded by your actions because in their mind they have a surrendered opponent. However, in this masquerade we are saving our energy and waiting our turn to create and implement a system that is empowering to our community.

In this embryonic stage, we have to enter into the local politics of our community. We have to take the majority of the city committee seats, as representatives of the four wards we will create a voting bloc, voting in the city council that represent each ward in our communities. Here we need a majority of 5 out of 7 to overrule any veto power the Mayor have, then directing our focus to the Mayor's office. As these representatives are put in power by us, we will DEMAND that they answer to us. Controlling the local laws that govern; from the local commerce to property taxes; from residential concerns to the application of law enforcement. Never conforming to this old system, but instead using it as a tool for our means of acquiring "Power". In essence becoming the Policy writers in our own communities. Economic independence is vital here.

This voting block is created at the grass root level. It is accomplished by bringing non-profit organizations together that serves the local community concerns. These groups coupled with the owners of the business systems, will become the engine that represent the community, Creating subdivisions in each part of the city, performing as the nerve center of that area. These chapters will be responsible for addressing the concerns of the elderly, from providing transportation services to making sure the basics are provided; from weekly clean-up activities to protecting our community from vultures. These small gestures will start a following. This following will be registered as voters, and the candidates that addresses and supports our needs will receive our support. At this stage, we will address our educational system, the allocation of our taxes, and the vision for our community. These few adjustments can create a degree of change that will allow us to have control of our community resources, educational, and training institutions where we will then produce, teach, and develop our future leaders.

The Political and Economic influence at lower levels must evolve by the acquisition of resources wherein we are able to own, and control production facilities. When we can control intricate parts of the economy, when we can employ thousands of people in this state, here we will have the type of power that is necessary to direct the political machine, and bring about the change we are discussing in this pamphlet.

On the State level of politics, this critical stage addresses the writing of Statues and laws that govern our daily lives [this is where our people are criminalized]. First by establishing enough economic and political power, we will rescind the laws that are bias towards our people. We will implement laws that will minimize the power the government has over our lives, and we will implement laws that assist our people in the advancement of our mission. This tactic must be practice with a clear understanding that the government is not our saver, but instead a tool to be used achieve our ultimate goals. "Wealth" and "Power" must be the ingredient used to secure our place in this world; from the local level, to the State level, from the National level, and ultimately to the international level.

There are many views over the years that have contributed to our struggle and our ultimate political aim. Some say return to Africa, others argued we must secure 5 states in the south of America as an independent nation for Black people, and still others say we must use the advancement of this system and create dual citizenship in West Africa for our children. This mission must be debated further.

It has been stated that, "the strong do what they want, and the weak suffer what they must." These few adjustments will begin a journey toward strength.

Greater details in the practical application of political struggle will be forthcoming in future pamphlets called <u>Urbanomics</u>". We will grow!

CHAPTER 6
THE ABILITY TO ACQUIRE POWER

How do you see your ability to make change and acquire power?

The answer to this question can only come from your mind [thought & strategy] and the endowment of self-awareness.

By keeping your mind on the positive, by counting your blessings, by believing in your abilities to accomplish anything, believing in the possibility of your own success. By creating short term and long term goals, and using your ability to be self-critical in analyzing your effectiveness, by focusing on your goals and them alone, we will create the mental state necessary to acquire "Power".

Your own character must be your source of strength. For it is in this state of being that your success is nurtured and allowed to come forward.

If you find yourself feeling that life is unfair, remember that as bad off as things may seem, you need only look to our history, and our forefathers who fought through slavery, and to our mothers who suffered through the daily rapes and brutalities during slavery, NOW envision their strength and the power of their metal fortitude that carried them through. Believing that if they hold fast a better day was ahead for their children. TRUE WARRIORS!

We are those children who now have to take this system by the horn and master its movements. It starts first in the mind knowing that we can and will win. Seeing opportunities everywhere, and where there is no opportunities: **MAKE OPPORTUNITIES!**

This calls for a level of mental and emotional maturity in order to see our mission through. In working towards our long term goals, we cannot get upset over the inevitability of minor setbacks. We must understand that setbacks or losses are a part of the learning process in life and the struggle towards acquiring "Power".

So failing at something is not something to be ashamed of. It is not a sin, nor is it an indicator of our abilities or the lack thereof. Failure is nothing more than proof of one's attempt to achieve. For me at least, failure would be the failure to pick yourself up, dust yourself off, and go at it all over again with the determination and the focus of an improved strategist, and warrior, with your actions saying with conviction that.. "Succumbing is not an option".

Remember: the only difference between a warrior and a defeated man is that a warrior goes ahead and does what defeated people just talks about doing.

There is an old saying that "Adversity has the effect of eliciting talents which, in prosperous circumstances, would have laid dormant." Other brothers would say struggle is ordained by God because it causes us to become immersed within ourselves, pinpointing the answers to our obstacles. In other words, sometimes in stumbling it brings out the very best in us.

Remember everyone's potential is limited only by what they believe their limitations to be. So believe your potential as a winner and your defined mission for the good of your family, our people, and communities. You can be whatever you want to be, and the only person who can stop you, and your ability to execute your mission is your submission to failures and the negative influence of others that do not believe in you, your abilities and your goals.

Protect your mind from the naysayers. This part is best accomplished by not telling others of your plans for success! The only people that should be privileged to your thoughts, ideas, and goals are members of your mastermind team.

In divulging others to your thinking, you're running the risk of not executing your goals. This is for two reasons. The first reason lies in the notion that if you speak on your plans to anyone outside of your team you will squander your desire to see it through, the logic is, just by mentioning your plans will give you a sense of success although you did nothing to see your plans manifested in the physical. The other reason is, people outside of your team will be haters for a thousand different reasons envy, jealousy, hate, greed… But whatever the reason, they will almost never be as enthusiastic about your plans, goals, or ideas as you are, and their lack of enthusiasm alone may be enough to kill your spirit & desire. This is where your character must be strong and your faith must come from within, and when you need affirmation or validation you have to turn to your master mind team who are supportive of your mission.

In choosing your team, it is important that you only welcome those into your circle that share in [y]our spiritual harmony, the defined goals and mission ascribed too, surrounding yourself with those that think, act, live, plan, and play on a different level than the average person. Whose thoughts are above the ordinary work a day thought pattern, those that has discovered how to increase the intensity of thought to the point of seeing the present circumstance saying it can't be done. Instead of functioning out of the negative scripts, opinions, and perceptions of others. We build the same mental wavelength that we are on.

To bring forth the creation we must sharpen the tools that are used to create and this is ourselves.

CHAPTER 7
CLOSING COMMENTS

This pamphlet was written to bring awareness in our community about my individual struggle and to where it is possible seek support in my cause for my right to be FREE, but just as important, it was written to make you the reader aware of the change that must occur to you or our children. It is each of our responsibility.

The message that I want to send from this pamphlet is change is possible, and the answers to changing our conditions lie dormant within us all. "He who conquers his/her internal nature is also able to achieve dominion over the external world." Therefore Political Power, and Economical Power will be a reflection of our self-Empowerment. Today my brothers & sisters, I salute you as the Creators of [y]our own lives. I look forward to the day that our people are empowered, controlling our own communities productively, being producers on the world stage instead of the target consumers of the market capitalist. I look forward to the day when we are a force to be reckoned with. Becoming players in politics and the writing of laws, and effectively using the tools of wealth and power to achieve our goals.

It has been said that too, "TREAT A MAN AS HE IS HE WILL REMAIN AS HE IS. TREAT A MAN AS HE CAN AND SHOULD BE AND HE WILL BECOME BETTER."

I hope my thoughts sparks conversations amongst the young and older, the educated class and the uneducated, the street thug and the 9-5 mothers and fathers. We are all in this together and the superficial titles need not keep us apart. I hope this is the beginning of some of the things we can all build on. I'll be speaking again in future installments with details on specific Topics. Until next time salutations and love.

"HOW TO"
A PRACTICAL APPLICATION
THIS INSTALLMENT IS ON LAW

*EXCERPTS ARE FROM THE
PRISONERS SELF HELP LEGAL CLINIC MANUAL

CHAPTER 8
ON LAW

So for starters to understand "The Rule of Law", I incorporated excerpts that address the practical application on how to go about addressing civil and criminal law in the courts. I have quoted in part, and added my own comments in part on the summarized excerpts from the [PSHLC] Manual. In pamphlets that will follow, I will address "how to" on all of the above topics of Power that we discussed.

WHY IS LEGAL RESEARCH IMPORTANT?

Because in this country our lives and liberties are on the line.

I do not offer the studying of law as a suggestion to be beggars of the courts for our rights, however my position is that every individual needs to master the law creating a level of consciousness in our communities of the tactics used against us. Formulating a state of awareness.

In this continued awareness, we have to find our strengths and make a clear objective assessment of our weaknesses. We need to assess "the powers that be" strengths and weaknesses. If this is not done, death and destruction of our bodies, minds, and spirits will be our continued path which leads to continued suffering.

*WHAT ARE YOUR RIGHTS?

"LAW" is not a science. It is a fluid, ever changing, combination of such things as statutes, rules, codes, regulations, cases and ordinances. Only by studying federal and state laws, and their judicial interpretation, can you understand your rights and if or how they have been violated.

*WHAT ARE YOUR REMEDIES?

Once you know something about what rights you have, you can then look to the "law" to see what types of relief you may have. This information is often spelled out in statues and judicial decisions. It is in this same area that we have to influence how the law is written.

*WHAT ARE THE PROCEDURES?

If you have been injured under the law, you will need to know what procedures you must follow to obtain relief. Generally, you must adhere to the procedures described in statues and regulations or in judicial decisions and carefully observe any time limitations. (NOTE: One man's death penalty appeal was not heard by the Supreme Court of Virginia because it was filled <u>one day late.</u>)

This, the goal of legal research is to educate the researcher, who may then use the full range of information available to effectively pursue his or her rights both as individuals and as a community.

ORGANIZING YOUR CASE FOR RESEARCH:

STATEMENT OF FACTS; the first thing in researching a potential violation of the law is to compose a <u>STATEMENT OF FACTS.</u> This statement tells the court <u>exactly </u>what has happened, and it also helps you focus your legal arguments. It should recount <u>accurately</u> and <u>factually</u> every significant event or development that has taken place concerning your action.

MOTIONS: The facts in a motion should be contained in the affidavit in the form of allegations. Use of fact for each allegation. It is important that only FACTS ABOUT WHAT HAS HAPPENED ARE INCLUDED IN THIS STATEMENT AND <u>NOT</u> OPINIONS, ACCUSATIONS, CONCLUSIONS, INTERPRETATIONS, OR JUDGEMENTS. This statement should accurately and concisely answer the questions <u>WHO, WHAT, WHEN, AND HOW</u> as to the parties and events involved in your case.

ESTABLISHING A CAUSE OF ACTION: After clearly stating the facts, go over your statement and attempt to formulate questions as to what you think your rights are and how these rights may have been violated. Try to make these questions simple and straight forward.

EACH RIGHT IS A CAUSE OF ACTION:

Separate <u>each</u> instance of a potential violation from your fact statement and attempt to specify which constitutional or statutory right you are claiming was violated. Remember, these must be facts to substantiate the claim. Sometime down the road you will be required to <u>PROVE</u> your allegations on the basis of evidence, that is, the facts.

Be certain that you can demonstrate the following:

*The facts in your statement or allegations are <u>true</u>.

*Your rights were violated under the Constitution or a statute.

*You suffered an injury or loss.

*The injury you suffered may be legally attributed to the specific acts (or failure to act) of others (the named defendants), who were required by law to do (or not do) those acts.

Being able to specify these issues in advance will greatly assist you in your initial research efforts. Of course, you may not clearly understand your rights, or even if you have any rights in the specific instance, until after you have done some research.

HOW TO USE A LAW LIBRARY:

You should understand from the outset that even the highest paid lawyers are not more able to find the law than you are. Their key advantage is that they have access to better facilities. Once you learn where the law is, it is merely a matter of reading it <u>carefully</u> and then arguing your points <u>clearly</u> and <u>succinctly.</u>

READING A BASIC CASE CITATION

Reading a basic case citation is relatively straight forward and simple for example, assume you are interested in the following case: <u>Valentine v. Beyer</u>, 850 F. 2d 951 (3D CR. 1988), this citation and case title contain the following information:

1. "F,2d" means that the opinion will appear in the Federal Reporter, Second Series and will report a decision of the Federal Appeals Court.
2. "850" means that the case will appear in volume #850 of the Federal Reporter, second series.
3. "951" means that the case will start on pages 951 of vol. 850 of the Federal Reporter.
4. "3rd. Cir." means that the case was decided by the United States Court of Appeals for the third Circuit.
5. "1988" means that the opinion was rendered in the year 1988.
6. The title of the case tells you that the first named party is the moving party that is either the plaintiff at the trial court level, or the appellant of petitioner at the appellate level. The name of the party appearing after the small"v" (versus) is the defendant at the trial court, or respondent or appellant at the appeals courts.

METHODS OF RESEARCH

There are three basic approaches to researching any legal problem:

1. Word or topic
2. Statute
3. Case

The one you use depends only on the type and amount of information you have to start with. The chief difficulty is making the proper initial diagnosis or classification of the field of law where your problem lies and seeing all of the potential issues. The more time you spend thinking out the problems and issues beforehand, the more time and effort you will save in the long run.

If you already have a case or statue that you can refer to, that is usually the easiest way to begin. However, if you know almost nothing about the subject area, you will have to begin by picking out a key word or phrase and looking that up in the research material listed below.

THE KEY WORD APPROACH

There are many sets of law books that access the law on a word or topic basis. For instance, West's N.J. Digest, West's Federal Digest, and <u>Corpus Juris Secundum</u> (CJS). These are encyclopedic multi volume sets of books containing commentaries on the law. Each of these sets has a "word index" some very detailed and some very general.

Next Steps

The Internet is a great tool for conducting your primary research. Simply type your interest into your favorite search engine... you will find plenty of information. Other resources at your fingertips are business publications. Many titles are available to assist you along the way.

<u>Let our mission began, and to those who have their own script, we say, no one way is the perfect way, it is only when we have the same purpose that we will meet on the road of success to fulfill our mission.</u>

"In one of the copies of my books is the code to win $1000- scan this code or go to my website, subscribe to my email list, and see if that's you"- Mr. Anthony Ways

http://www.anthonywaysjourney.com